SQUIRES KITCHEN'S GUIDE TO MAKING

iced flowers

Ceri DD Griffiths

Piped and stencilled sugar flowers for cakes, cookies and desserts

First published in September 2012 by
B. Dutton Publishing Limited, The Grange,
Hones Yard, Farnham, Surrey, GU9 8BB.
Copyright: Ceri DD Griffiths 2012
ISBN-13: 978-1-905113-37-8

Publisher: Beverley Dutton

Group Editor: Jenny Stewart

Art Director/Designer: Sarah Ryan

Editor: Jenny Royle

Designer: Zena Manicom

Graphic Designer: Louise Pepé

Copy Editor: Amy Norman

Editorial Assistant: Frankie New

Photography: Alister Thorpe

Printed in China

Wallpapers supplied by wallpaperdirect.co.uk

Disclaimer

The Author and Publisher have made every effort to
ensure that the contents of this book, if followed carefully,
will not cause harm or injury or pose any danger. Please
note that some inedible items, such as flower stamens
and cake dowels, have been used in the projects in this
book. All such inedible items must be removed before the
cake is eaten. Similarly, any non food-grade equipment
and substances, such as non-toxic glue, must not come
into contact with any cake or cake covering that is to be
eaten. Neither the Author nor the Publisher can be held
responsible for errors or omissions and cannot accept
liability for injury, damage or loss to persons or property,
however it may arise, as a result of acting upon guidelines
and information printed in this book.

introduction

I graduated as a Master Baker and Confectioner in 1980, and in the following years I worked within the baking industry both in the UK and abroad where my style developed into what it is today.

During my years of training, royal icing was the most popular choice for cake decoration and I thrived on the challenges this versatile medium offered me. When I started to design this book I decided early on that I wanted to give royal icing a facelift and offer exciting projects with a contemporary twist. You won't find a single traditional royal-iced cake within these covers and that was a deliberate decision on my behalf. I believe the way forward is to create designs that use royal icing creatively alongside a variety of other mediums.

This book contains iced flowers for both the beginner and advanced sugarcrafter; I hope these skills become the first step on a path that will lead you to a long love affair with royal icing.

I hope you get as much pleasure from making iced flowers as I do.

acknowledgements

A huge thank you goes to my mother
and sister who put up with my sugary
lifestyle; Stef, Rachel and Lucy for their
unconditional friendship; Jacqui Kelly for
being my sounding board; my unofficial
assistant, Jane; and Alan Dunn who
introduced me to Beverley and Rob
Dutton. And last but by no means least,
all the team at B. Dutton Publishing
and Squires Kitchen for allowing me to
explore my love of cake artistry.

contents

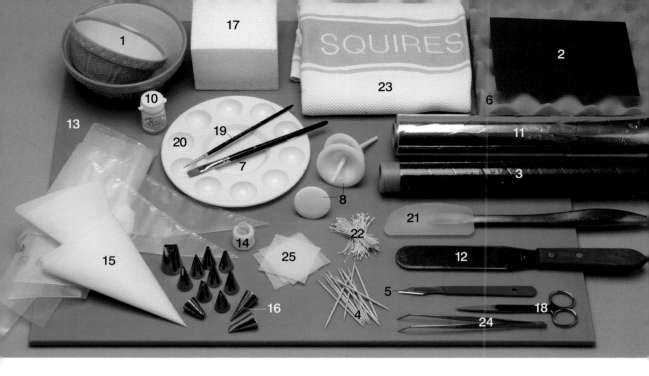

essential equipment and edibles

When creating iced flowers, it is important to have everything you need to hand before you begin. Due to the speed at which royal icing dries, you do not have the luxury of time that you have when creating sugarpaste flowers. Before you start, make sure that you go through all the stages for creating the flower you wish to produce and take note of the edibles and equipment you will need. By doing so you will be able to make sure you have all the materials and equipment ready before you start. Having everything prepared means that you will be able to relax and enjoy creating your iced flowers.

Below is the basic equipment you will need for making the iced flowers in this book.

equipment

1 Bowls for storing royal icing

2 Card or acetate for making stencils

3 Cling film

4 Cocktail sticks

5 Craft knife

6 Dimpled foam

7 Dusting brush

8 Flower nail: flat or lily nail (depending on the flower)

9 Food mixer strong enough to make royal icing (not pictured)

10 Glaze Cleaner (SK)

11 Kitchen foil

12 Large palette knife

13 Non-stick board

14 Nozzle adaptor (optional)

15 Plastic, parchment or silicone piping bags

16 Piping nozzles: I have used PME Supertubes nos. 1, 2, 3, 4, 13, 44, 50, 51, 56, 57 and 57S, and Wilton 124 and 104 in this book

17 Polystyrene block

18 Scissors

19 Small paintbrush

20 Small paint palette for mixing colours

21 Spatula

22 Stamens

23 Tea towel

24 Tweezers

25 Wax paper

parts of a petal nozzle

All instructions given within this book are for right-handed pipers, however piping in the opposite direction (for left-handed pipers) will achieve the same flower.

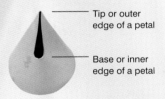

Tip or outer edge of a petal

Base or inner edge of a petal

It is important to note that there are three basic types of petal nozzles available and they are marked R, L, or S. Nozzles marked with an R are for right-handed pipers, those marked with an L are for left-handed pipers and those marked with an S are straight and therefore suitable for all pipers. Some brands have no markings at all so check with your supplier before you buy.

Left   Straight   Right

Although iced flowers do not require too many different edible materials, there are a few essentials that you will always need. Royal icing, liquid or dust food colours, edible pollens, edible glue and confectioners' glaze are some of the basics that you will need to create each flower. If you are piping roses, depending on the size of the rose, you will also require Sugar Florist Paste, cornflour and white vegetable fat. Any specific requirements are given at the beginning of each project.

edibles

1 Cornflour

2 Confectioners' Glaze (SK)

3 Dust Food Colours (SK)

4 Edible Glue (SK)

5 Liquid Food Colours (SK)

6 Metallic Dust Food Colours (SK)

7 Pollen-style Food Colours (SK)

8 Instant Mix Royal Icing (SK)

9 Sugar Florist Paste, SFP (SK)

10 White Vegetable Fat

tutor tip

If you choose to dust your royal iced flowers when they are dry, it is best to dust them prior to arranging them on your cake. Do not dust your flowers if you want to store them for later use, as the colour may fade over time.

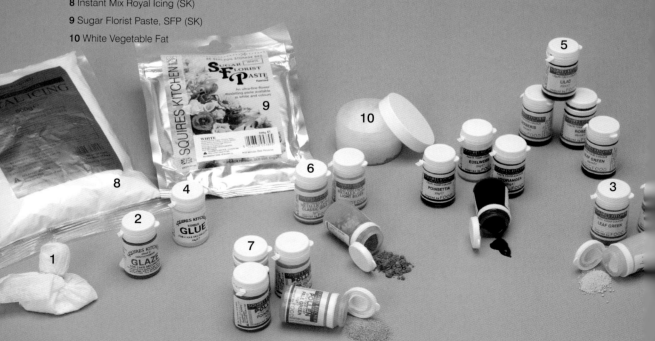

working with royal icing

how to make royal icing

I used Squires Kitchen's Instant Mix Royal Icing for all the flowers and projects in this book. The advantage of using a pre-mix is that, if you follow the instructions on the packet, your royal icing will be the right consistency every time. Always sieve any pre-mix thoroughly prior to use to distribute the ingredients evenly as this will help you to achieve the same consistency each time.

Run-out icing

If you would like to make your own royal icing, you can follow this basic recipe.

edibles

455g (1lb) icing sugar

15g (½oz) SK Fortified Albumen powder

Cooled, boiled water

equipment

Small bowl

Weighing scales

Sieve

Mixer

Spatula

Makes 455g (1lb) royal icing

1 Reconstitute the albumen powder as per the instructions on the pack.

2 Weigh and sieve the icing sugar.

3 Place ¾ of the icing sugar into the mixing bowl, lower the K beater into it and switch the mixer on at a slow speed. Add ¾ of the reconstituted albumen.

4 As the royal icing mixes, check the consistency: if it appears to be thick and syrupy then add a little more icing sugar; if it appears to be dry and crumbly, add a little more reconstituted albumen.

5 Periodically stop the mixer and scrape down the inside and bottom of the

Soft-peak icing

Firm-peak icing

mixing bowl with a spatula so that there are no pockets of unmixed icing sugar.

6 Once the royal icing is approximately the right consistency (i.e. similar to a thick cake batter) increase the speed on the mixer. After a few minutes the icing will become whiter in colour and fluffier in texture.

7 When the royal icing is white and fluffy, take it off the mixer and beat it by hand as this will help you judge its consistency. Achieving the correct consistency of royal icing will come with practice, however you are aiming to mix the icing so that it holds a firm peak when you lift away from the icing with a palette knife. At this point you can adjust the consistency for the project you are working on by adding more reconstituted albumen or sieved icing sugar.

tutor tip

Always ensure all the equipment you use to weigh, make, handle, pipe and store the royal icing has been washed thoroughly in hot, soapy water to remove any traces of grease. If any grease gets into royal icing it will make it unusable.

storing royal icing

1 When you've finished working with your bowl of royal icing, scrape the sides of the bowl down and smooth the icing to a flat surface.

2 Using a clean, damp cloth wipe the insides of the bowl. This is important because if there is any icing on the sides of the bowl and it crusts over, it can drop into your royal icing and block piping nozzles when you are piping.

3 Place a piece of cling film directly onto the surface of the royal icing. Make sure there are no air pockets and that the cling film is also in contact with the inside of the bowl.

4 Lay a clean, damp cloth or tea towel over the top of the bowl and set aside.

5 When you use royal icing after storage you do not need to re-mix it in a machine; beating it by hand using a spatula will be enough to re-establish the consistency of the royal icing.

Storing royal icing varies depending upon the climate you live in. I don't need to store my royal icing in a fridge, but it is essential if you live in a hotter climate. If you do have to refrigerate your royal icing, always let it come back up to room temperature before you use it.

Personally, I don't keep my royal icing for more than three days as I like to use it fresh. However, as a general guideline, I would not recommend keeping royal icing for more than five days as after this time the structure begins to weaken and the egg albumen may go off.

using colour with royal icing

Colour is a wonderful element when designing cakes and its clever use will set your creations above all others, adding that elusive 'wow' factor.

If you are making a cake for someone you know or as a commission, the colours you use will normally be dictated by the client; however, a basic knowledge of colour balance is essential for pleasing – and in some cases, dramatic – effects in cake design. One of the best pieces of equipment for use in cake design is an artist's colour wheel: this small, readily available reference guide will show at a glance how monochromatic, complementary and contrasting colours in different shades and tones can enhance the overall impact of your design.

When colouring royal icing, only liquid or dust food colours are generally recommended. Paste food colours that contain glycerine (also known as glycerol) and glycerides should be avoided for royal icing as they will prevent the icing from fully drying. However, it is worth noting that all paste food colours in the Squires Kitchen range do not contain glycerine and are suitable for use with royal icing.

Liquid food colour is perfect for pastel or normal colouration, however for deep colours such as red, black, deep purple and royal blue the use of dust food colour is essential. Adding too much liquid colour will change the consistency of the icing, making it too fluid to work with. When using dust food colours it is best to colour a small portion of

royal icing as it will take a lot of dust food colour to get the intensity of a strong colour. Making intensely coloured royal icing 24 hours prior to its use will prevent the appearance of spots on your wet royal icing caused by the particles of dust colour dissolving at different rates. I would recommend only using intensely coloured royal icing for accent pieces and line work, rather than for more prominent features on a cake. There is the possibility these colours will bleed into surrounding paler colours over time, so these accents should be added to your creation last.

One final note on the use of colour on cakes: colour can be very significant for the recipient of the cake. If you are making cakes for sale or for someone you don't know directly, always ask questions concerning colours and their meaning at the consultation stage of cake designing, before you start work on the cake. Colours can also evoke emotions and preconceived imagery so it is wise to be aware of these when designing a cake for a specific event. The following are a few examples of meanings associated with colours:

Blue – calmness, dignity

Black – elegance, rebellion

Green – freshness, naturalness

Purple – royalty, sophistication

Red – excitement, danger

White – purity, kindness

Yellow – joy, reminiscence

using a piping bag

Once you have made and coloured the royal icing as required, you will need to use it in a piping bag (unless you are making stencilled flowers such as the poinsettia, poppy or orchid). To use a piping bag:

1 If you are using a parchment paper bag, snip off approximately 1.3cm (½") from the tip. Place the required piping nozzle into a piping bag so that the tip of the nozzle protrudes from the end.

2 Hold the bag in one hand and use a palette knife to ²/₃ fill the bag with royal icing.

3 Fold the top of the bag over away from the seam, then fold the corners in (like an envelope) to seal the top of the bag and push the icing to the end to expel any air.

4 Hold the bag near the tip and squeeze with your thumb and index finger until the icing comes out. Support the bag with your other hand as you pipe.

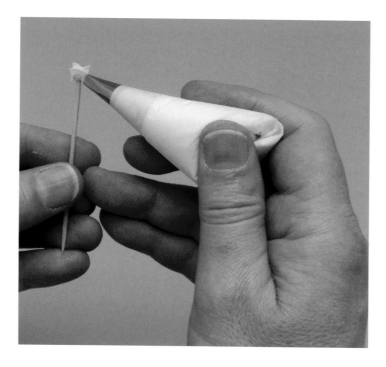

top tips on royal icing

- Use freshly made royal icing whenever possible, as this will give you better results when making iced flowers.

- Always keep the end of your piping nozzle clean as this will make it easier to control when piping.

- When using royal icing, your best friend is a slightly damp, fine-tipped paintbrush as you can use it to reposition icing without having to re-pipe the decoration.

- When dusting royal icing with food colour, the fine blending of colour can only be achieved if you are using a dust colour fractionally lighter or darker than the iced flower you are working on.

- By filling a piping bag with two similar colours of royal icing, you will be able to create unique two-toned flowers which will not need dusting.

- With iced flowers, always remember the phrase 'less is more'. Do not colour up a large batch of royal icing for flowers as a little goes a long way.

- Do not worry about trying to match the colour of your subsequent batches of royal icing to your original icing colour. As long as you are using the same food colour, any variations will only add interest to your finished flowers, giving them a more natural-looking colour range.

covering a cake

Before you decorate a celebration cake you will need to coat it, either with royal icing or sugarpaste (rolled fondant). If you are using a rich fruit cake it should be covered with marzipan first, then either sugarpaste or royal icing following the two different methods described below. Sponge cakes are usually crumb-coated with a thin layer of buttercream or ganache, then coated with sugarpaste (this is much quicker than coating with royal icing).

Once your cake is covered it is ready to be decorated with beautiful iced flowers or any other decoration of your choice.

how to sugarpaste a rich fruit cake

edibles

Rich fruit cake

SK Marzipan

Apricot glaze

Icing sugar shaker

Clear spirit

Sugarpaste

equipment

Large, serrated knife

Cake drum or board

Sieve

Pastry brush or palette knife

Non-stick board (optional)

Non-stick rolling pin

Marzipan spacers (optional)

Sharp knife

Ruler

Smoother

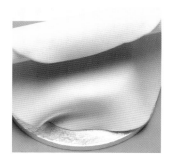

1 Prepare the fruit cake by levelling it with a large, serrated knife. Roll a sausage of marzipan to go around the edge of the cake, cut a neat join then turn the cake upside down. Fill any air pockets or holes with small pieces of softened marzipan if necessary. Place the cake onto a cake drum or board ready for the marzipan covering.

2 Sieve the apricot jam then boil it to make a glaze (this also destroys any bacteria present). Using a pastry brush or palette knife, brush the top and sides of the cake with the glaze whilst it is still warm.

3 Dust a work surface or non-stick board with sieved icing sugar to prevent sticking and knead the marzipan to soften it. Roll out the marzipan to a thickness of approximately 7mm (¼"), ensuring that it is large enough to cover the top and sides of the cake in one go. If you have marzipan spacers these can be used to give the marzipan a uniform depth.

4 Cover the top and sides of the cake with one piece of SK Marzipan in preparation for the sugarpaste, using the rolling pin to lift the paste onto the cake. Smooth the marzipan over the top and sides using the palm of your hand, then finish with a smoother. Trim away any excess paste at the base.

5 Use a pastry brush to dampen the surface of the marzipan with clear spirit (such as gin or vodka) or cooled, boiled water if preferred. This will make the surface slightly tacky, helping the sugarpaste to stick.

6 Using the same method as for coating the cake in marzipan (described in steps 3 and 4 above), coat the cake with sugarpaste. To prevent air bubbles from forming under the paste, smooth the surface from the centre of the cake outwards and down the sides. Use a smoother to create a level, polished finish and trim neatly at the base with a sharp knife.

tutor tip

Should an air pocket appear between your paste and the coating beneath, use a sterilized pin to pierce it and release the air. Gently rub the paste in a circular motion until the pinhole disappears and store the pin safely away from the cake.

how to sugarpaste a sponge cake

edibles

Sponge cake
Buttercream or ganache
Icing sugar shaker
Clear spirit
Sugarpaste

equipment

Large, serrated knife
Cake drum or board
Sieve
Pastry brush
Non-stick board (optional)
Non-stick rolling pin
Marzipan spacers (optional)
Sharp knife
Ruler
Smoother
15mm (½") width ribbon
Non-toxic glue stick or dress pin

1 Layer and coat the sponge cake with buttercream or ganache. Use a palette knife or side scraper to smooth all the surfaces and to remove any excess filling: the smoother the surfaces the better your final coating of paste will be.

2 Dust a work surface or non-stick board with sieved icing sugar to prevent sticking and knead the sugarpaste to soften it. Roll out the sugarpaste to a thickness of approximately 7mm (¼"), ensuring that it is large enough to cover the top and sides of the cake in one go. If you have marzipan spacers these can be used to give the sugarpaste a uniform depth.

3 Coat the cake with sugarpaste in one piece, working from the centre of the cake outwards and down the sides, smoothing as you go. It is important to try and avoid creating air pockets between the paste and the coating underneath. Should an air pocket appear, use a sterilized pin to pierce it (see tip on page 15).

4 Use sugarpaste smoothers to obtain a smooth, polished finish and trim neatly around the base with a sharp knife.

5 If the board/drum on which the cake is placed is bigger than the cake, take the sugarpaste down onto the cake drum then smooth and trim neatly around the edge. To cover the cake board/drum separately roll out the sugarpaste into a long, narrow strip that is long enough to go around the circumference of the cake. Cut one long edge straight.

6 Dampen the exposed board/drum with a little cooled, boiled water. Place the sugarpaste onto the board with the straight edge against the cake, overlap the ends and trim the join neatly. Smooth the surface and trim around the edge with a sharp knife. If the cake and board are square, cover each side separately and smooth the joins at the corners.

7 Trim the edge of the board/drum with coordinating 15mm (½") width ribbon. Secure in place using either a non-toxic glue stick or double sided tape.

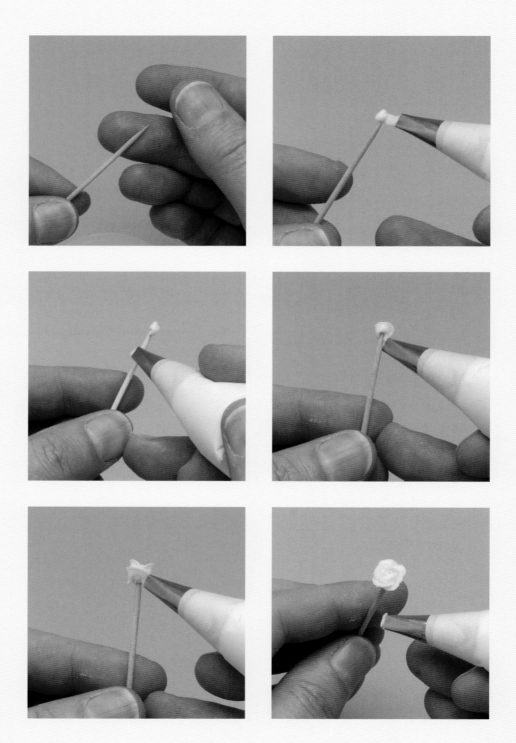

mini roses

edibles

SK Instant Mix Royal Icing

SK Professional Liquid Food
Colour of your choice

SK Professional Dust Food
Colour of your choice

White vegetable fat

equipment

Cocktail sticks

Piping bags

Piping nozzle: no. 56 (PME)

Small palette knife

Polystyrene block

Dusting brush (SK)

1   Smear a little white vegetable fat onto the top section of a cocktail stick then wipe off the excess.

2   Colour some soft peak white royal icing using the liquid food colour of your choice. Fit a silicone piping bag with a no. 56 petal nozzle and then fill the bag to $^2/_3$ full with the coloured royal icing.

3   Line up the piping nozzle with the tip of the cocktail stick and apply pressure to the icing bag until the royal icing attaches to the cocktail stick. Once the royal icing is attached to the cocktail stick, keep piping to create a ribbon of icing. Turn the cocktail stick in an anticlockwise direction (clockwise if you are left-handed) and wrap the ribbon of icing around the cocktail stick to form a bud.

4   When you have created a rose bud, stop piping and bring the end of the royal icing ribbon down to the cocktail stick beneath the bud to finish.

5   Using an arching motion starting and ending beneath the bud, pipe three overlapping petals around the bud. Turn the cocktail stick as you work and pipe the petals towards you. You may wish to finish the rose at this stage, in which case skip to step 7.

6 Using an arching motion again, starting and ending beneath the first three petals, pipe five overlapping petals around the outside; this time pipe these petals away from you. This completes the mini open rose.

7 These mini roses can be left on the cocktail sticks to dry: push the end of the cocktail stick into a block of polystyrene and allow to dry. As long as the cocktail sticks are greased with white vegetable fat first the roses should come off easily once the icing is dry. If your royal icing is a little soft, push the cocktail stick through a square

of wax paper then pull through so that the rose attaches to the paper and set aside to dry. Once dry, carefully remove the cocktail stick or wax paper.

8 When the roses are dry, dust them with a coordinating dust food colour using a dusting brush. Concentrate the colour towards the centre of the rose to give a more realistic effect.

9 Pipe the calyx onto the back of the rose when you are ready to attach it to the cake, cookie, etc. (see instructions on page 93); this will hold the rose in place.

mini roses

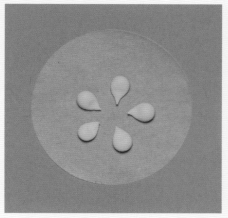

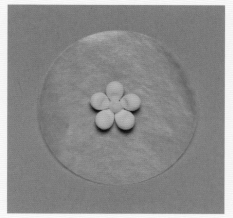

teardrop flowers

edibles

SK Instant Mix Royal Icing

SK Professional Liquid Food
Colours: Daffodil (yellow) or
Sunflower for centres and a
petal colour of your choice

SK Professional Dust Food
Colour of your choice

equipment

Piping bags

Piping nozzle: no. 2 (PME)

Small palette knife

Wax paper

Fine tweezers

Fine paintbrush (SK)

1 Colour some soft peak white royal icing using the liquid food colour of your choice. Fit a silicone piping bag with a no. 2 nozzle and fill the bag to $^2/_3$ full with the coloured royal icing.

2 Using the pressure piping method, pipe rows of teardrops onto wax paper, aiming to make them all roughly the same size. If you have not pressure piped before, place the nozzle onto the paper, squeeze to form a bulb and gently pull down to make a teardrop.

3 Leave these individual petals to dry for several hours before removing them from the wax paper. These can either be used immediately or stored for later use.

4 To pipe the centre and build the flower, colour some soft peak white royal icing using Daffodil or Sunflower liquid food colour. Fit a silicone piping bag with a no. 2 nozzle and fill the bag $^2/_3$ full with the coloured icing.

5 Pipe a small bulb of the yellow royal icing onto a square of wax paper or directly onto the cake where you want the finished flower to sit. It is sometimes difficult to create these flowers directly on the side of a cake, therefore assembling them on wax paper and letting them dry before affixing them to the cake is usually easier.

6 Use a pair of tweezers to insert five individual petals into the yellow icing bulb which forms the centre of the flower, then use a fine paintbrush to adjust the position of the petals. These flowers dry in approximately half an hour.

cameo cookies

Serving up these individual works of art will put you on the map as the queen of afternoon tea, or the king of cookies.

iced flowers

Piped mini roses (between 2 and 7 per cookie), see pages 20 to 23

Piped teardrop flowers (between 3 and 4 per cookie), see pages 24 to 25

edibles

Cookies of your choice

SK Modelling Cocoform: White

Sugarpaste: duck egg blue

SK Instant Mix Royal Icing

SK Professional Liquid Food Colours: Daffodil (yellow), Leaf Green, Nasturtium (peach), Rose

SK Professional Dust Food Colours: Chestnut (soft beige), Daffodil (yellow), Rose

SK Professional Metallic Lustre Dust Food Colour: Classic Gold

SK Confectioners' Glaze

SK Edible Glue

Icing sugar for dusting

equipment

Oval and rectangular cutters

Rolling pin

Piping bags

Piping nozzles: nos. 2, 3, 50 (PME)

Paintbrushes: small dusting brush, small glue brush, small round brush (SK)

SK Glaze Cleaner (IPA)

1 Create an array of mini roses and teardrop flowers from royal icing in a colour scheme to match your chosen occasion. I used Daffodil, Nasturtium and Rose coloured icing dusted with Daffodil, Chestnut and Rose dust colours.

2 Bake a batch of cookies using your favourite recipe and cut to shape: I chose ovals and rectangles (then cut off the corners) but cameo cookies can be made in various shapes. Hearts lend themselves perfectly to piped flower sprays. Allow to cool completely.

3 Roll out the paste then cut it to shape using a smaller size cutter than you used to make the cookie. Use a fine coating of edible glue to

attach a thin layer of White Cocoform or duck egg blue sugarpaste to the top of your cookies.

4 Fit a silicone piping bag with a no. 3 nozzle then ²/₃ fill the bag with royal icing coloured with Daffodil liquid food colour. Pipe a small shell border around the oval of White Cocoform.

5 Fit a silicone piping bag with a no. 2 nozzle then ²/₃ fill the bag with white royal icing. Pipe rows of dots around the oval of duck egg blue sugarpaste. If the dots have peaks caused by the piping nozzle, touch them down with a damp paintbrush.

6 When the shell border around the oval of Cocoform is completely dry, paint it using a fine paintbrush and a mixture of confectioners' glaze and gold metallic lustre dust. Clean your paintbrush immediately afterwards with glaze

cleaner, then rinse in clean water to preserve your paintbrush.

7 Prior to attaching your flowers to the cookies it is a good idea to arrange them on a clean work surface; this will allow you to play around with the eventual design. Having a paper template of the cookie shapes will also aid you with this.

8 Fit a silicone piping bag with a no. 50 leaf piping nozzle then ²/₃ fill the bag with royal icing coloured using Leaf Green liquid food colour. Attach the piped flowers to the sugar cookies with piped leaves (see page 93) then set aside for a couple of hours to dry.

9 Arrange the cookies on a pretty plate or stand. As a delicate finishing touch you may wish to add a large sugar rose to your display (see instructions on page 37).

medium roses

edibles

SK Sugar Florist Paste (SFP) in
the colour of your choice

SK Instant Mix Royal Icing

SK Professional Liquid Food
Colour of your choice

SK Professional Dust Food
Colour of your choice

equipment

Cocktail sticks

Piping bags

Piping nozzle: no. 57 (PME)

Small palette knife

Dusting brush (SK)

Wax paper

1 Colour some soft-peak white royal icing using the liquid food colour of your choice. Fit a silicone piping bag with a no. 57 petal nozzle and then fill the bag ²/₃ full with royal icing.

2 Create a small teardrop of SFP in your chosen colour and push it onto the tip of the cocktail stick.

3 Line up the piping nozzle with the base of the SFP teardrop and apply pressure to the icing bag until the royal icing attaches to the teardrop. With the royal icing still attached, keep piping to create a ribbon of icing. Turn the cocktail

stick in an anticlockwise direction (clockwise if you are left-handed) then wrap this ribbon around the SFP teardrop to form a bud.

4 When you have created a rose bud, stop piping and bring the end of the royal icing ribbon down to the cocktail stick beneath the bud to finish.

5 Using an arching motion starting and ending beneath the bud, pipe three overlapping petals around the bud. Turn the cocktail stick as you work and pipe the petals towards you.

6 Using an arching motion again, starting and ending beneath the first three petals, pipe five overlapping petals around the outside; this time pipe these petals away from you. You may wish to finish the rose at this stage, in which case skip to step 8.

7 Add a further seven petals in the same way around the outside of the rose to make a fully open rose, if desired.

8 Push the cocktail stick through a square of wax paper so that the rose can be removed and set aside to dry. Once the rose has been left to

dry for 24 hours, remove the wax paper square and place the rose upside down on a piece of food-grade foam sponge so that the SFP teardrop can also dry completely.

9 When the roses are dry, dust them with a coordinating dust food colour using a dusting brush. Concentrate the colour towards the centre of the rose to give a more realistic effect.

10 Pipe the calyx onto the back of the rose when you are ready to attach it to the cake (see instructions on page 93); this will hold the rose in place.

chocolate and roses

Nothing says "I love you" more than a long stemmed red rose. Who wouldn't fall in love with someone if that rose was delivered with a rich, creamy chocolate dessert?

edibles

Mikado biscuit sticks (or similar)

SK Instant Mix Royal Icing

SK Professional Dust Food Colours: Berberis (ivory), Nasturtium (peach), Poinsettia (Christmas red)

SK Professional Liquid Food Colour: Leaf Green

SK Milk Belgian Chocolate Mousse

SK Chocolate Ganache Mix

SK Edible Gold Leaf or fresh mint leaves

equipment

Large Savoy piping bag

Large Savoy star piping nozzle

Piping nozzles: nos. 51, 57 (PME)

Silicone piping bags

1 Colour the royal icing either red or orange. To obtain an intense colour it is best to use Poinsettia dust food colour for the red roses and a mixture of Nasturtium and Berberis for the orange.

2 Fit a silicone piping bag with a no. 57 nozzle then 2/3 fill the bag with red or orange royal icing. Following the instructions on pages 30 to 33, pipe a medium rose onto a biscuit stick (you do not need to create a small teardrop of SFP at the beginning as the biscuit will support the rose and do not place the rose onto wax paper at the end). Allow to dry.

3 Following the instructions on the packaging, make up the chocolate mousse and place it into serving dishes. Leave in the fridge to firm.

4 Make up a batch of chocolate ganache using the instructions on the packet. When cool and firm, whisk it up to make a chocolate buttercream.

5 Fit a Savoy piping bag with a large Savoy star piping nozzle and fill with the chocolate buttercream. Pipe a swirl of chocolate buttercream into the dishes on top of the chocolate mousse.

6 Push a long stemmed rose into the chocolate dessert and garnish with a touch of edible gold leaf or a couple of fresh mint leaves.

large roses

edibles

SK Sugar Florist Paste (SFP) in
the colour of your choice

SK Instant Mix Royal Icing

SK Professional Liquid Food
Colour of your choice

SK Professional Dust Food
Colour of your choice

White vegetable fat

Cornflour

equipment

Cocktail sticks

Large piping bags

Piping nozzle: no. 124 (Wilton)

Paintbrushes: dusting brush,
round brush (SK)

Small palette knife

Polystyrene block

1 Rub a little white vegetable fat onto the top section of a cocktail stick; this will ensure the rose will come off easily when dry. Create a teardrop of SFP and push the cocktail stick into the base to form the base shape for the bud. Set this aside for 24 hours to dry completely before piping.

2 Fit a silicone or nylon piping bag with a no. 124 petal nozzle, then $^2/_3$ fill the bag with royal icing coloured with the liquid food colour of your choice. Holding the cocktail stick between your thumb and index finger, roll the cocktail stick in an anticlockwise direction (or clockwise if you are left-handed). At the same time touch the

nozzle on the base of the teardrop shape then pipe a ribbon of royal icing around in a spiral to form a bud. To achieve the required shape, bring the piping nozzle up, towards you and then down.

3 Using the same motion as described in step 2, touch the petal nozzle on the base of the bud and then pipe three overlapping petals towards yourself in an arching motion. Using a dry paintbrush dusted with cornflour, shape these petals and tidy up the base of your rose to keep it rounded. It is wise at this stage to leave your rose to dry for several hours so that the weight of the petals still to be piped will not misshape your finished rose.

4 When the centre of your three-petal rose is dry hold the cocktail stick between your thumb and index finger. Touch the petal nozzle on the base of the three-petal rose. Roll the cocktail stick in a clockwise direction (anticlockwise if you are left-handed) and pipe five overlapping petals away from yourself in an arching motion. Using a dry paintbrush dusted with cornflour, shape these petals and tidy up the base of your rose. If possible, leave your rose again to dry for several hours to prevent it from becoming misshapen. For a half-open rose, leave to dry for 24 hours then skip to step 6.

5 Using the same method of piping as for the previous petals, add a further seven overlapping petals if desired, always remembering to shape and tidy them as you go.

At this point leave your rose to dry for 24 hours before proceeding onto the last steps.

6 Once the rose is completely dry it can then be dusted using dust food colours. For a realistic effect, catch the colour on the edges of the petals and use more colour towards the centre of the flower. Gently pass the rose through the steam from a kettle to set the dust: this will cause the surface to appear shiny at first but it will dry to a matt finish in approximately 15 minutes. The rose can then be removed from the cocktail stick with a slight twisting motion.

7 If you are making large roses for a cake, pipe the calyx onto the back of the rose to attach it to your cake (see page 93).

tutor tip

Large piped roses can be used to decorate a small cake, a dessert or a plate of cookies as shown on page 28.

To impress your guests, simply add a few pre-iced roses to freshly baked macaroons. The sweet crunch of the royal icing will offer the perfect contrast to the delicious chewiness of the macaroon.

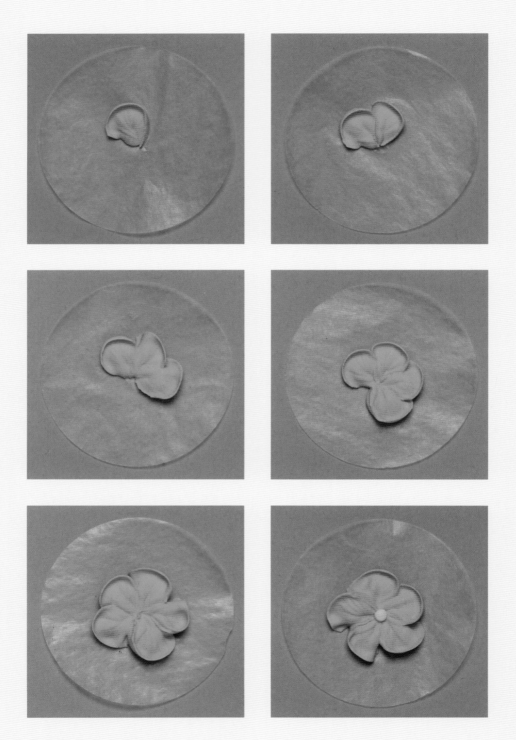

five-petal blossom

five-petal blossoms

edibles

SK Instant Mix Royal Icing

SK Professional Liquid Food Colours: Daffodil (yellow) for centres and a petal colour of your choice

SK Professional Dust Food Colour of your choice

equipment

Piping bags

Piping nozzles: nos. 1, 56 (PME)

Small palette knife

Flower nail

Wax paper

Round paintbrush (SK)

1 Fit a silicone piping bag with a no. 56 petal nozzle (or a larger petal nozzle if required). Colour some royal icing with your chosen liquid food colour then fill the bag to ²/₃ full with the royal icing.

2 Attach a square of wax paper to the head of a flower nail using a small touch of royal icing.

3 Holding the flower nail between your thumb and index finger, roll the nail in an anticlockwise direction (or clockwise if you are left-handed). At the same time pipe a small arch with the petal nozzle to create an individual petal, ensuring that you start and finish in the centre of the nail. Keep the arch narrow: there should be no gap in the centre of the petal.

4 Continue to pipe the petals round in a circle from the same central point. It is important to stop between each petal as this will give your final

flower more definition. When you pipe the fifth and final petal, finish it by lifting the piping nozzle directly upward and then position the edge of the last petal against the first using a dry paintbrush.

5 Whilst the blossom is still wet, tidy up its centre with a dry paintbrush. Lift the square of wax paper off the head of the flower nail and set it aside to allow the flower to dry.

6 To finish the blossom, colour a small amount of soft peak white royal icing using Daffodil liquid food colour. Fit a silicone piping bag with a no. 1 nozzle and fill it ²/₃ full with the yellow royal icing. Pipe a small bulb in the centre of the flower where the petals meet to represent the blossom's centre. If the nozzle leaves a peak of icing, touch the centre down with a damp paintbrush. Leave the blossom to dry completely before removing it from the wax paper square.

country baskets

These delightfully simple cupcakes topped with tasty marzipan flavours and miniature fabric bows would be a hit at any country fair or bake sale.

iced flowers

Piped five-petal blossoms (10 per cupcake), see pages 40 to 41

edibles

Vanilla cupcakes baked in SK Dotty Cupcake Cases: Spring Green

Vanilla buttercream

SK Instant Mix Royal Icing

SK Professional Liquid Food Colours: Daffodil (yellow), Leaf Green, Marigold (tangerine), Nasturtium (peach), Sunflower

SK Sugar Florist Paste (SFP): Pale Yellow

SK Instant Marzipan Mix: Hazelnut & Orange, Almond & Apricot or Apple & Cinnamon

SK Edible Glue

Icing sugar for dusting

equipment

Basket weave rolling pin or impression mat

Dresden or flower shaping tool

Non-stick board

Non-stick rolling pin

Piping bags

Piping nozzles: nos. 50, 56 (PME)

Small palette knife

Round cutter to match the diameter of your cupcakes

Small paintbrush

Small, sharp knife or cutting wheel

Food-grade plastic bag

Dresden modelling tool or cocktail stick

Kitchen paper or drinking straw

1 Using a piping bag fitted with a no. 56 nozzle, make around 120 small five-petal blossoms following the instructions on page 41 (you will need approximately ten blossoms per cupcake). To make the spring colours shown here use white, Daffodil, Marigold, Nasturtium and Sunflower coloured royal icing.

2 Bake the cupcakes and when cool, hollow out the centre and fill with vanilla buttercream.

3 Mix up a batch of the Instant Mix Marzipan in the flavour of your choice. Dust a work surface with icing sugar, roll out the marzipan and texture it using a basket weave rolling pin or texture mat. Select a round cutter that matches the diameter of your cupcakes and cut out discs of the textured marzipan. Using

a thin coating of buttercream, attach a disc of marzipan to the top of each cupcake.

4 Fit a silicone piping bag with a no. 50 leaf nozzle. Fill the bag to ²/₃ with royal icing coloured using Leaf Green liquid food colour.

5 Attach the blossoms to the cupcakes with piped leaves (see page 93), making sure that the leaves do not protrude over the edge of the cupcake case if you are displaying them in cupcake wrappers.

6 To finish the cupcakes create a small fabric bow using SFP following the instructions below and stick one to the centre of each cupcake using edible glue. Place the cupcakes into wrappers for display if you wish.

mini bows

These little sugar bows look gorgeous on cupcakes and cookies and can be made to coordinate with the colour of your flowers. They are easy to make and you can prepare them in advance ready to pop on a finished piece.

1 Thinly roll out a small piece of SFP using a non-stick rolling pin and board. The thinner the paste is rolled the more natural the folds in the bow will appear: as a guide, if you can see the colour of your board through the SFP then it is thin enough. I have left my bows plain, however if you wish to create a fabric effect on the bow you can either roll the paste with a textured rolling pin or gently press a texture mat onto the surface.

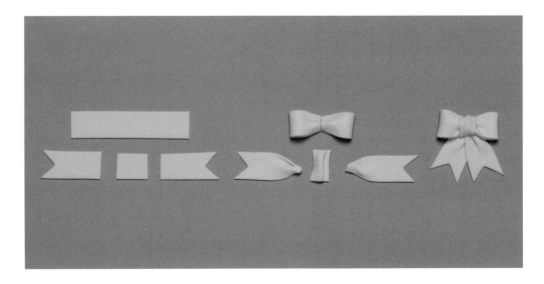

2 Cut out the bow pieces using a sharp knife or a cutting wheel. Follow the step-by-step photograph as a guide or use the template given on page 94. Place all of the pieces under a sheet of food-grade plastic (such as a freezer bag) while they are not in use to prevent them from drying out.

3 Take the longest strip of SFP (this will eventually form the loops of the bow) and slightly moisten it at its central point using a paintbrush dampened with cooled, boiled water or edible glue. Fold the two ends to the middle and gently pinch together; this is where the knot piece will eventually be wrapped. Use two small pieces of kitchen paper or a drinking straw inserted into the loops to keep them open whilst they dry.

4 Take the two tail pieces of SFP with the forked ends and pinch the blunt end of each to make a pleat. Immediately attach these two tail sections to each other with edible glue. Remember that bows look more realistic with pleats and folds.

5 Take the remaining piece of SFP and gently squeeze it to create a slight pleat down its length. Dampen the back of the bow looped piece of SFP in the centre and wrap the knot around it, pressing gently at the back to secure it in place. Glue the bow and knot on top of the tails.

6 Whilst the SFP is still soft, use a Dresden modelling tool or a cocktail stick to add extra markings to the knot, loops and tails, giving the impression of further pleats in the bow. Once the SFP has dried completely, remove the loop supports.

topiary cake pops

Perfect for any occasion from a children's birthday party to an elegant wedding reception, your guests won't be able to resist the urge to eat these sugary sweet flowers, then enjoy the tasty bite-sized treat beneath.

iced flowers

Piped five-petal blossoms (approximately 30 per cake pop), see pages 40 to 41

edibles

Cake pop mixture (cake crumbs mixed with buttercream)

SK Instant Mix Royal Icing

SK Professional Liquid Food Colours: Daffodil (yellow), Lilac, Nasturtium (peach), Rose, Sunflower

SK Professional Dust Food Colours: Daffodil (yellow), Lilac, Nasturtium (peach), Rose, Sunflower

SK Easy Melt White Chocolate Flavoured Coating

equipment

Bowl for melting the Easy Melt Coating

Lollipop sticks

Piping bags

Piping nozzle: no. 56 (PME)

Polystyrene block

Decorative ribbon

1 Fit a silicone piping bag with a no. 56 petal nozzle then fill the bag $2/3$ full with royal icing coloured using the liquid food colour of your choice. To make the cake pops shown here I used five different liquid colours as listed above to make a pretty pastel palette. Following the instructions on pages 40 to 41, pipe several small five-petal blossoms. You will require approximately 30 blossoms per cake pop depending on their size.

2 Create a batch of cake pops using your favourite recipe; I use approximately one part buttercream to three parts cake crumb. Chill your cake pop mixture at each stage of production so that it holds its shape.

3 Melt the Easy Melt chocolate coating and divide it into bowls, one for each colour. Add a dust colour to each bowl, either to match the colour of the blossoms or in a contrasting colour to add a little drama! Roll the cake pop mixture into balls, dip the end of the lollipop sticks into the melted coating and push the balls onto the sticks. Dip the cake pops into the melted chocolate and allow to dry by pushing the sticks into a polystyrene block.

4 When the coating has completely set, use dots of royal icing the same colour as the blossoms to attach them to the cake pop. Insert them back into the polystyrene block and leave to set completely for a couple of hours so that the blossoms do not get dislodged in transit.

5 For a final finishing touch, tie a small ribbon bow around the cake pop stick.

These pretty pastel cake pops make stunning wedding favours if coloured the same as the bride's bouquet and then finished with a complementary bow to match the wedding dress. These can then be presented in a clear cellophane bag tied with a coordinating ribbon.

azaleas

edibles

SK Instant Mix Royal Icing

equipment

Piping bags

Piping nozzles: no. 44 (PME);
no. 104 or 124 (Wilton)

Small palette knife

Kitchen foil

Lily nail

Round paintbrush (SK)

Dimpled foam or cupped former

Stamens: white (optional)

Tweezers (optional)

1 Fit a plastic or nylon piping bag with a no.
124 petal nozzle for large azaleas or a no.
104 for smaller azaleas. Fill the bag to ²/₃ with white
royal icing.

2 Cut a square of kitchen foil and insert it into a
lily nail ensuring that the shiny surface is facing
upwards. Wrap the outer edges over the lip of the
nail as this will help hold the foil in place when piping.

3 Start piping a petal down inside the lily
nail, moving upwards to the lip and back
down again. The petal will naturally frill, however to
accentuate the frill you can move the piping nozzle
back and forth as you pipe.

4 Continue to pipe all five petals individually.
Piping all the petals in one motion will
build up too much icing at the base of the flower,
lengthening the drying time and reducing the
depth of the trumpet, so always ensure that you
stop piping after each petal.

5 Once you have piped five petals to create
the azalea, use a dry paintbrush to smooth
over the joins at the base of the petals and
remove any excess royal icing. Gently lift the foil
and flower out of the lily nail and set it aside to
dry on dimpled foam or in an empty egg carton.
These flowers will take approximately a week to
dry thoroughly.

6 When the azaleas are completely dry gently peel the foil away from the flower. Fit a silicone piping bag with a no. 44 star nozzle (or a star nozzle appropriate to the size of your azaleas), and fill the bag ²/₃ full with the royal icing. Pipe a small cone of royal icing into the centre of the azalea. To further enhance the azalea, stamens can be pushed into the wet royal icing using tweezers, although it is worth cutting the number of stamens required to size before adding them. Remember that if you do add stamens they must not be eaten, so it is important to inform the recipient of the cake before serving so that the flowers can be removed safely.

tutor tip

If you wish to make an azalea without stamens, pipe the centre in pale yellow royal icing using the no. 44 star nozzle.

azalea waterfall

The combination of sugarpaste and royal icing on this imposing wedding cake will give your guests a variety of flavours and textures. However you show them off, I can guarantee these azaleas will be the incredible sugar flowers that everyone talks about.

iced flowers

28 piped azaleas, see pages 49 to 51

edibles

12.5cm, 18cm and 23cm (5", 7" and 9") round cakes covered with cream sugarpaste (see pages 14 to 17)

SK Instant Mix Royal Icing

SK Bridal Satin Lustre Dust Food Colour: Double Cream

SK Professional Liquid Food Colour: Leaf Green

SK Edible Glue

equipment

12.5cm and 18cm (5" and 7") round cake cards

30.5cm and 35.5cm (12" and 14") round cake boards (drums) covered with cream sugarpaste and trimmed with cream satin ribbon (see page 17)

Plastic cake dowels

Craft knife

Flat dusting brush

Piping nozzles: nos. 44, 52, (PME); 104 (Wilton)

SK Great Impressions Small Lace Scroll Mould

Stamens: white (optional)

1 Using your favourite recipe, bake the three tiers for this wedding cake. Prepare each one following the guidelines on pages 14 to 17 and place the middle and top tiers onto thin cake cards of the same size. Coat the cakes and boards/drums with cream sugarpaste. To support the tiers when stacked, insert four dowels into the bottom tier. Push each dowel down to the board at the bottom then mark level with the sugarpaste coating. Remove the dowels, cut them to size using a craft knife then re-insert them into the cake. Repeat with the middle tier then carefully stack all three tiers.

2 Roll out the sugarpaste trimmings into a long strip and use the lace scroll mould to emboss the paste. Use a sharp knife or cutting wheel to cut out a long sugar ribbon. Dust this ribbon with Double Cream Bridal Satin Dust then attach it around each cake using edible glue.

3 Fit a silicone piping bag with a no. 52 leaf piping nozzle, then $^2/_3$ fill the bag with royal icing coloured using Leaf Green liquid food colour.

4 Build a waterfall of piped azaleas down one side of the wedding cake, attaching the

flowers with piped leaves (see page 93). Pipe the leaves sparingly as the wet royal icing could soften the sugarpaste coating on the wedding cake and weaken the support required for the azaleas. Work from the top tier down to the base board.

5 Leave the completed wedding cake overnight to allow the royal icing to dry completely before transportation; this will help to prevent any damage to the flowers due to movement. The flowers can be supported with small pieces of food-grade foam sponge or kitchen paper until dry, however ensure they are removed once the cake is at the venue.

tutor tip

Instead of piping the leaves, you could use an SK Great Impressions leaf mould with green SFP to create non-wired realistic leaves to accompany your azaleas.

poppies

edibles

SK Instant Mix Royal Icing

SK Professional Dust Food
Colours: Blackberry (black),
Poinsettia (Christmas red)

equipment

Card or thin plastic for stencils

Rose petal cutter or template
(see page 94)

Craft knife

Wax paper

Dimpled foam

Piping bag

Piping nozzle: no. 44 (PME)

Round paintbrush (SK)

Pointed tweezers (optional)

1   Make your own stencils for the poppy petals
    from card or plastic by drawing around a
rose petal cutter or using the template on page 94.
Once you have drawn the outline, carefully cut it
out with a craft knife.

2   Make up a small batch of royal icing and
    colour it using Poinsettia dust food colour to
achieve the intensity of colour required.

3   Cut squares of wax paper large enough
    for your petals and then spread the royal
icing through your stencil using a piece of card or
plastic. Gently lift the stencil away from the wax

paper to give a clean edge to your petal. Whilst
the icing is still wet, lay the wax paper on dimpled
foam: this will give each petal a slight curve so that
your finished poppy does not look completely flat.

4   The petals will dry fairly quickly, however I
    recommend leaving them for several hours
to dry completely before dusting the pointed part of
the petals with Blackberry dust food colour.

5   When assembling the poppies there are
    two options: you can either construct them
directly on the cake, or make them on a small
square of wax paper to be attached when fully

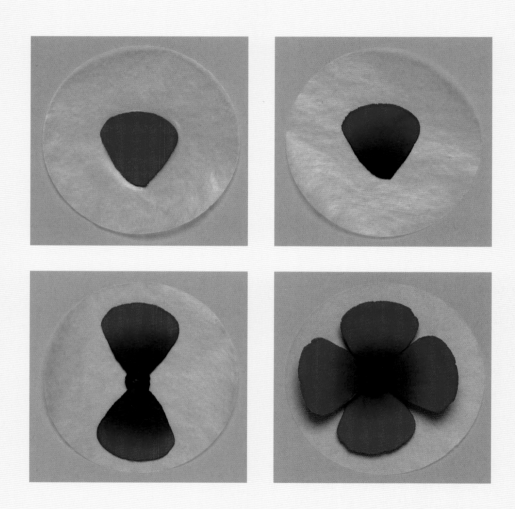

dry. Colour a small amount of royal icing black with Blackberry dust food colour and pipe a bulb with a no. 44 nozzle onto either the cake or wax paper. Attach two opposite petals to this bulb, pipe another small bulb of black onto the join and then attach the other two petals. When they are secured pipe a larger, flatter bulb with the no. 44 nozzle to create the centre of the poppy. Use a dry paintbrush to manipulate the petals if needed.

6   These poppies are very fragile so must be handled carefully. If you have made them on wax paper, use a pair of tweezers to pick them up by their centres and attach them to the cake with a small bulb of royal icing.

poppies

meadow wedding

Simple and chic, the meadow daisy and poppy complement each other perfectly. This stunning wedding cake is designed for a couple who want something uniquely inspired by nature.

iced flowers

7 stencilled poppies, see pages 55 to 57

21 piped daisies, see pages 62 to 63

edibles

15cm, 20.5cm and 25.5cm (6", 8" and 10") square cakes covered with pale green sugarpaste (see pages 14 to 17)

SK Instant Mix Royal Icing

SK Professional Liquid Food Colour: Leaf Green

SK Professional Dust Food Colours: Blackberry (black), Poinsettia (Christmas red)

SK Pollen Style Edible Dust Food Colour: Pale Yellow

SK Edible Glue

equipment

15cm and 20cm (6"and 8") square cake cards

35.5cm (14") square cake boards (drums) covered with pale green sugarpaste

Plastic cake dowels

15mm (½") and 25mm (1") width satin ribbon: pale lime

Piping bags

Piping nozzles: nos. 4, 44, 57 (PME)

Dusting brush (SK)

Pointed tweezers (optional)

Wax paper

1 Using your favourite recipe, bake the three tiers for this wedding cake. Prepare each one following the guidelines on pages 14 to 17 and place the middle and top tiers onto thin cake cards of the same size. Coat the cakes and boards/drums with sugarpaste coloured with a hint of Leaf Green liquid food colour and trim the base board with pale lime ribbon (see page 17).

2 To support the tiers when stacked, insert four dowels into the bottom tier. Push each dowel down to the board at the bottom then mark level with the sugarpaste coating. Remove the dowels, cut them to size using a craft knife then re-insert them into the cake. Repeat with the middle tier then carefully assemble the cake so that each tier is stacked directly above the other at the front right-hand corner.

3 Attach a length of wide, pale lime-coloured satin ribbon around the base of each tier and secure the ends to each other (not the cake) with double-sided tape. Trim the base board with the 15mm (½") width ribbon in the same colour.

4 Colour some royal icing using Leaf Green liquid food colour to match the shade of your cake as closely as possible. Fit a silicone piping bag with a no. 4 piping nozzle then ²/₃ fill the bag with the pale green royal icing. Pipe curls and swirls directly onto the side of the cake; drawing them first onto a piece of paper will help you decide on the overall design. Where necessary, use a damp paintbrush to tidy up the ends of the piped lines.

5 Pipe approximately 21 daisies using the instructions on pages 62 to 63, and attach them to the wedding cake when dry with small bulbs of white royal icing. Place more daisies towards the base of the cake to balance the overall design.

6 Carefully attach seven stencilled poppies to the wedding cake using firm-peak royal icing coloured leaf green to match the coating of the cake.

For complementary macaroon wedding favours see pages 64 to 65.

These striking red poppies come in a variety of different colours in nature, so don't be afraid to adjust their colouring to suit your project. If you add another petal to these poppies you can create five-petal fantasy flowers that would be great for decorating any cakes, cookies or desserts.

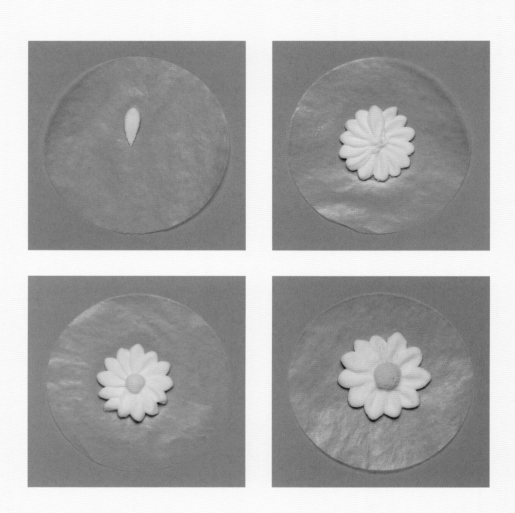

daisies

edibles

SK Instant Mix Royal Icing

SK Professional Liquid Food
Colour: Daffodil (yellow)

SK Pollen Style Edible Dust
Food Colour: Pale Yellow

equipment

Piping bags

Piping nozzles: nos. 3, 57S
(PME)

Wax paper

Flower nail

Round paintbrush (SK)

1 Fit a silicone piping bag with a 57S petal nozzle (or a different size depending on how big you would like your daisies to be). Fill the bag ²/₃ full with white royal icing. Note that you will be holding the bag with the petal nozzle opposite to normal so that the base (widest part) of the nozzle will create the outside edge of the teardrop-shaped daisy petal.

2 Attach a square of wax paper to the head of a flower nail using a small touch of royal icing.

3 Holding the flower nail between your thumb and index finger, pipe a long teardrop of royal icing with the straight petal nozzle to create an individual petal, ensuring that it finishes in the centre of the nail. Continue to pipe petals to the same central point, keeping the outside edge of the flower circular.

4 Pipe as many petals as required to complete the head of the daisy (usually around 13 or 14) then use a dry paintbrush to make sure that the centre of the daisy is smooth and that all of the petals meet in the middle.

5 Lift the square of wax paper with the daisy off the flower nail and set it aside to dry.

6 When the petals are fully dry, add the centre of each daisy. Colour a small amount of soft-peak royal icing yellow using Daffodil liquid food colour. Fit a silicone piping bag with a no. 3 nozzle and fill it ²/₃ full with the coloured royal icing. Pipe a bulb in the centre of each daisy then, whilst the icing is still wet, sprinkle it with Pale Yellow edible pollen dust. Leave the daisy centre to dry completely before shaking off the excess pollen, then remove the daisy from the wax paper square.

daisy macaroon favours

Crisp and crunchy with a hint of chewiness, these little wedding favours will make your guests smile. Colourful macaroons are the perfect complement to any event and can be decorated using any of the piped flowers in this book to suit your theme or celebration.

iced flowers

Piped daisies (1 per macaroon), see pages 62 to 63

edibles

SK Instant Macaroon Mix

SK Instant Mix Royal Icing

SK Professional Dust Food Colour: Leaf Green

SK Professional Liquid Food Colour: Leaf Green

equipment

Savoy piping bag

Piping nozzles: no. 4 (PME); Savoy round

Cellophane bags

Decorative lace ribbon

1 Make a batch of pale green macaroons from the macaroon mix, following the instructions on the packet. Colour the macaroon mixture using Leaf Green dust food colour before baking.

2 When the macaroons have cooled, sandwich them together with the filling of your choice.

3 Fit a silicone piping bag with a no. 4 piping nozzle then 2/3 fill the bag with royal icing coloured using Leaf Green liquid food colour to match the shade of your macaroons. Pipe a spiral onto the top surface of the macaroon.

4 Attach a piped daisy to the top of each macaroon with a small bulb of white royal icing and leave to dry for several hours. It is not advisable to pipe the daisies directly onto the macaroons as the moisture from the wet icing could cause them to soften.

5 Place two or three macaroons into clear cellophane bags and tie with a lace ribbon for presentation.

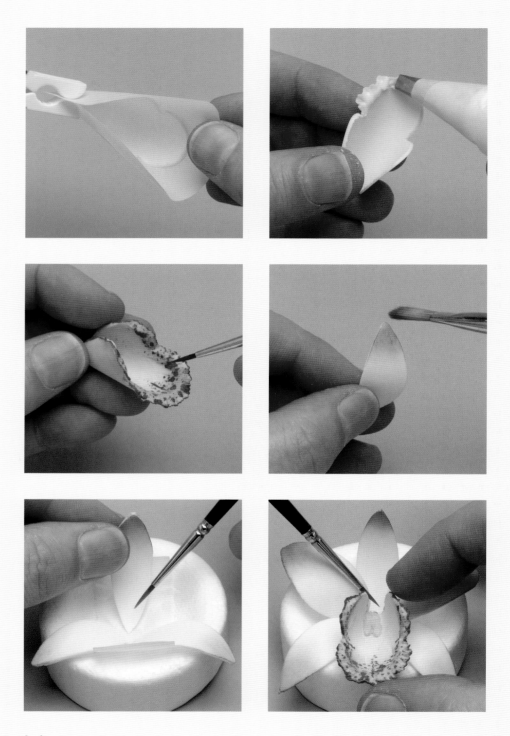

orchid

edibles

SK Instant Mix Royal Icing

SK Professional Dust Food
Colour of your choice

SK Professional Liquid Food
Colour of your choice

SK Pollen Style Edible Dust:
Pale Yellow

equipment

Card or thin plastic for stencils

Orchid cutters or template (see
page 94)

Craft knife

Wax paper

Curved formers such as a rolling
pin and apple tray

Peg or clip

Piping bag

Piping nozzles: nos. 2, 56 (PME)

Small palette knife

Paintbrushes: dusting brush,
round brush (SK)

Kitchen foil or flower former

Food-grade foam sponge
pieces or kitchen paper

1 Make your own stencils for the orchid petals from card or plastic by drawing around a set of orchid cutters or using the templates on page 94. Once you have drawn the outlines, carefully cut them out with a craft knife.

2 Make up a small batch of royal icing and colour it as required using either dust or liquid food colour.

3 Cut pieces of wax paper large enough for the individual petals then spread the royal icing through your stencils onto the paper using a piece of card or plastic. Gently lift the stencil away

from the wax paper to leave a clean edge. To give the petals a smooth finish, use the surface that is attached to the wax paper as the front (top) surface when the wax paper is removed. Whilst the icing is still wet lay the wax paper over a curved surface. The top sepal should eventually curve towards the front when assembled and therefore should be dried over a curve such as a rolling pin. The other sepals and petals will eventually curve away from the front therefore they should be dried curving in the opposite direction such as the inside of an apple tray.

4 To make the throat of the orchid, stencil the shape onto wax paper then bring the ends

together with the icing on the inside. Secure the ends of the wax paper together with a peg or clip as shown. The throat is extremely fragile and difficult to remove from the wax paper; therefore it is wise to make several spares.

5 The sepals and petals will dry to the touch fairly quickly, however I recommend leaving them for several hours to dry completely before peeling the wax paper away from the back of the petals.

6 Once all of the pieces of the orchid are safely removed from the wax paper, fit a silicone piping bag with a no. 2 nozzle and fill the bag $2/3$ full with royal icing the same colour as your orchid. Pipe two lines of icing into the throat of the orchid and immediately sprinkle them with Pale Yellow edible pollen dust. Leave this to dry for a few minutes then gently shake out the excess pollen.

7 Fit a silicone piping bag with a no. 56 nozzle and fill the bag $2/3$ full with royal icing the same colour as your orchid. Very carefully pipe a frill along the edge of the orchid's throat to create the labellum, then use a lightly dampened paintbrush to blend the frill into the throat. Set aside to dry for approximately one hour.

8 Using a small dusting brush and the dust food colour of your choice, shade the individual parts of the orchid. When the throat of the orchid is dry, add dots of liquid food colour with the tip of a cocktail stick where desired and dust the frill to match the rest of the bloom.

9 To assemble the orchid create a small dish shape of kitchen foil or use a flower former, then place a small disc of wax paper in the base. Fit a silicone piping bag with a no. 2 nozzle and fill the bag to $2/3$ with royal icing the same colour as your orchid. Pipe a bulb of royal icing onto the disc of wax paper and position the sepals into it. Using a small, dry paintbrush ensure that the royal icing is in full contact with the sepals and is supporting them. Small pieces of foam or kitchen paper can be used for support whilst drying. Leave to dry for a while so that when you move onto the next stage you will not dislodge them.

10 Pipe a bulb of royal icing into the centre of the sepals and position the throat and petals into the icing. Use a paintbrush to ensure that the royal icing is in full contact with the stencilled pieces and is supporting them. Again, use small pieces of foam or kitchen paper for support whilst drying if needed. Leave for 24 hours to dry.

11 When the orchid is completely dry use a small dusting brush to colour any royal icing that is not shaded at the base of the petals and throat to match the rest of the orchid. Gently remove the flower and wax paper from the former, remove the wax paper and attach the orchid in place with a small bulb of royal icing. The completed orchid is exceedingly fragile, so attach the orchid to the cake at the venue if the cake is to be transported some distance. It is also a good idea to make spares of all the pieces to allow for breakages.

exotic elegance

Delicate, dainty and exotic this royal iced orchid makes a breathtaking centrepiece to a celebration cake at any event. The beauty of such an eye-catching flower is that the other decoration on the cake can be kept very simple.

iced flowers

1 stencilled orchid, see pages 66 to 69

edibles

15cm (6") square cake covered with white sugarpaste (see pages 14 to 17)

SK Instant Mix Royal Icing

SK Professional Paste Food Colour: Rose

SK Bridal Satin Lustre Dust Food Colours: White Satin

SK Edible Glue

equipment

23cm (9") square cake drum/board covered with white sugarpaste and trimmed with pink ribbon (see page 17)

Fine-tipped round paintbrush (SK)

Set of orchid cutters (optional)

Small glue brush

Sharp knife or cutting wheel

SK Great Impressions Small Lace Scroll Mould

1 Bake, prepare and coat your cake as required then cover with white sugarpaste (see pages 14 to 17). Place centrally on a cake drum/board and trim the edge of the boards with pink satin ribbon.

2 Knead together the sugarpaste trimmings from the cake and colour half the paste with Rose paste food colour to create a complementary pink tone. Roll out the paste, cut a long ribbon and wrap it around the bottom edge of the cake. Attach it in place with edible glue.

3 Roll out the remaining white sugarpaste and use the lace scroll mould to emboss the surface. Use an orchid cutter of your choice or a sharp knife to cut out three petal shapes per corner. Dust these petal shapes using SK White Satin lustre dust.

4 Attach the petal shapes to the corners of the cake using edible glue. If you wish to carry the textural interest to the top of the cake, the orchid can be placed upon a square or disc of textured paste.

5 Attach a single iced orchid to the centre of the cake with a small bulb of royal icing. These orchids are very fragile, therefore if you have to deliver the cake it may be wise to attach the orchid at the venue and have a spare as back up.

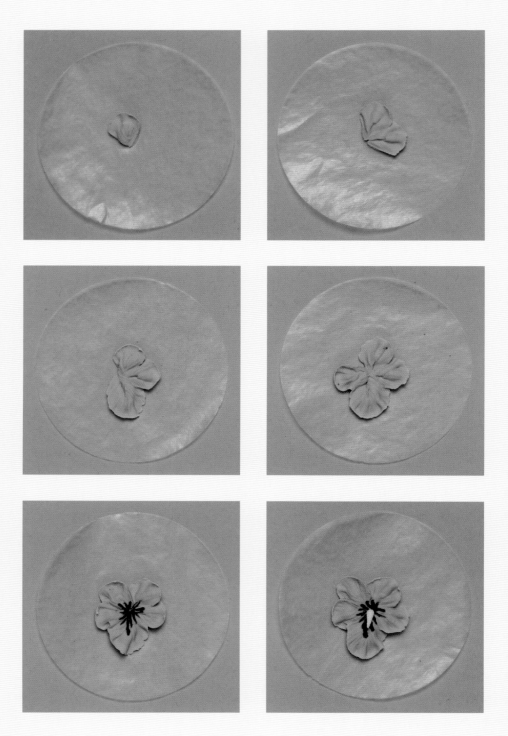

violets

edibles

SK Instant Mix Royal Icing

SK Professional Liquid Food
Colours: Daffodil (yellow), Violet
(purple)

equipment

Piping bags

Piping nozzles: nos. 1, 56
(PME)

Wax paper

Flower nail

Fine paintbrush (SK)

1 Colour some royal icing purple using Violet liquid food colour. Fit a silicone piping bag with a no. 56 petal nozzle and fill the bag ²/₃ full with the coloured royal icing.

2 Attach a square of wax paper to the head of a flower nail using a small touch of royal icing.

3 Hold the flower nail between your thumb and index finger and roll the nail in an anticlockwise direction (or clockwise if you are left-handed). At the same time pipe a small arch with the petal nozzle to create an individual petal, ensuring that you start and finish at the centre of the nail. It is important to stop between each petal as this will give your final flower more definition. Pipe the first and second petals the same size, pipe the third petal slightly longer and then pipe petals four and five the same size as the first two. When you pipe the fifth and final petal, finish it by lifting the piping

nozzle directly upward, then use a dry paintbrush to position the edge of the last petal against the first.

4 Whilst the violet is still wet, tidy up its centre with a dry, fine paintbrush. Lift the square of wax paper off the head of the flower nail and set it aside to allow the violet to dry.

5 Once the violet is dry, paint fine lines radiating from its centre using a fine paintbrush and Violet liquid food colour.

6 Colour a small amount of soft-peak royal icing using Daffodil liquid food colour. Fit a silicone piping bag with a no. 1 nozzle and fill it to ²/₃ full with the yellow royal icing. Pipe a small beak in the centre of the violet pointing down the length of petal three; this will represent the stamen. Leave the violet to dry completely before removing from the wax paper square.

lemon dress-up

Perfect for the host or hostess in a hurry, with a pre-piped stash of royal icing flowers you will be able to dress up any dessert instantly. In this project I turned a simple store-purchased lemon cheesecake into a dessert you could expect in any restaurant and your guests need never know.

iced flowers

Piped violets (approximately 4 to 6 per serving), see pages 72 to 73

edibles

Lemon cheesecake

SK Instant Mix Royal Icing

SK Professional Liquid Food Colours: Daffodil (yellow), Violet (purple)

SK Crystallized Natural Violet Fragments

Large lemon

Granulated sugar

equipment

Piping bag

Piping nozzles: nos. 1, 56 (PME)

Sharp knife to prepare the strips of lemon zest

Small saucepan

Wax paper

1   Either make or purchase a lemon cheesecake and slice into servings for your guests.

2   Use no. 56 petal nozzle and Violet coloured royal icing to make enough violets for your guests.

3   Cut thin strips of lemon zest from a fresh lemon, making sure to remove any white pith from the skin. Cutting the strips from the top of the lemon to the base will make them curl nicely when finished.

4   In a saucepan heat one part water and two parts granulated sugar and bring to a gentle boil. Add the lemon strips and reduce the mixture to a simmer. Continue to simmer until the water and sugar mixture starts to thicken. Cooking time will be approximately 15 minutes.

5   Carefully remove the strips from the pan (remember that they will be extremely hot) and spread them out on a sheet of wax paper. Try to separate them as much as possible so they do

not clump together. When cold they will add zing to your cheesecake.

6 Just before serving your dessert take a slice of lemon cheesecake and create a little nest of the crystallized lemon zest on top. Generously sprinkle with Crystallized Natural Violet Fragments and add a few of the piped violets for crunch.

tutor tip

This idea works equally as well using different citrus fruits such as orange, lime or grapefruit flavoured cheesecakes and coloured blossoms.

hydrangeas

edibles

SK Instant Mix Royal Icing

SK Professional Liquid Food
Colour: Hydrangea

SK Professional Dust Food
Colour: Hydrangea

equipment

Small palette knife

Piping bags

Piping nozzles: nos. 1, 56
(PME)

Wax paper

Flower nail

Paintbrushes: dusting brush,
round brush (SK)

Air puffer (optional)

1 Colour some firm-peak white royal icing using Hydrangea liquid food colour. Fit a silicone piping bag with a no. 56 nozzle and fill the bag ²/₃ full with the coloured royal icing.

2 Attach a square of wax paper to the head of a flower nail using a small touch of royal icing. Pipe four equal-sized petals in the same way as for the five-petal blossom (see page 41); this will form one of the many individual flowers within the head of the hydrangea. Whilst the individual flower is still wet, tidy up its centre with a dry paintbrush. Lift the square of wax paper off the head of the flower nail and set it aside

to allow the flower to dry. Repeat this until you have the required amount of individual flowers for your hydrangea: I have used approximately 12 to 15. It is best to allow the individual flowers to dry overnight before moving onto the next stage of the hydrangea.

3 When the individual flowers are completely dry dust their centres with Hydrangea dust food colour using a small, round dusting brush. This will add a further dimension to the finished hydrangea. Use an air puffer or soft brush to remove any excess dust colour and prevent it falling onto your cake.

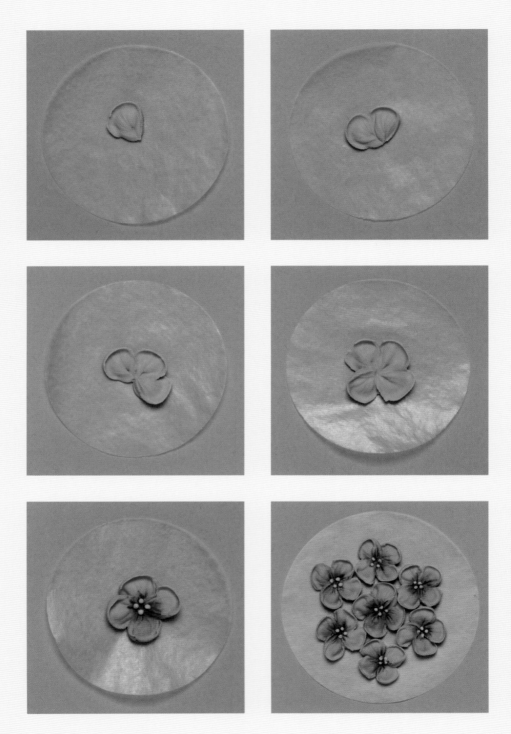

4 To finish the individual flowers, colour a small amount of soft-peak royal icing with Hydrangea liquid food colour. Fit a silicone piping bag with a no. 1 nozzle and fill it ²/₃ full with the coloured royal icing. Pipe four small dots in the centre of each individual flower where the petals meet to represent the stamens.

5 The hydrangea can either be assembled directly onto the cake or cupcake, or finished on a larger piece of wax paper, left overnight to dry then stored and used when required. To assemble the finished hydrangea fit a silicone piping bag with a no. 56 nozzle and fill it ²/₃ with Hydrangea coloured royal icing. Start by creating an outer circle of individual flowers. Using the petal tube to stick the flowers in place means that the finished hydrangea will have the illusion of extra flowers deeper within the finished bloom. Build up a dome of individual flowers by layering and decreasing the flowers until you place one final flower in the centre.

butterfly heaven

Nostalgic afternoon tea in the garden is a great time to reminisce with friends and family; these pretty little cupcakes will set your table apart from the rest and will give your guests a sweet treat to remember.

iced flowers

Hydrangeas (approximately 15 per cupcake), see pages 77 to 79

edibles

Flavoured cupcakes of your choice

Flavoured buttercream of your choice

Sugarpaste: white

SK Instant Mix Royal Icing

SK Professional Liquid Food Colours: Hydrangea, Leaf Green, plus colours of your choice for the butterflies

SK Professional Dust Food Colour: Hydrangea

Icing sugar for dusting

equipment

SK Cupcake Cases: Spring Green (or a colour of your choice)

Cupcake wrappers: butterflies (optional)

Piping bags

Piping nozzle: nos. 1, 2, 3, 56 (PME)

Non-stick board

Non-stick rolling pin

Round cutter to match the diameter of your cupcakes

Paintbrushes: small dusting brush, small round brush (SK)

Butterfly wing template (see page 94)

Thin card or plastic for templates

Thin card for wing formers

Wax paper

Stamens for butterflies (optional)

Craft knife

1 Colour some firm-peak royal icing using Hydrangea liquid food colour. Fit a silicone piping bag with a no. 56 nozzle and fill the bag to $2/3$ with the turquoise coloured royal icing. Following the instructions on page 77, create the individual flowers of a hydrangea.

2 Bake as many cupcakes as required and fill with buttercream when cool.

3 Dust a work surface with icing sugar then roll out some sugarpaste coloured pale green using Leaf Green liquid food colour. Select a round cutter that matches the diameter of your cupcake and cut out discs of the green sugarpaste. Attach the disc of sugarpaste to the top of the cupcake using buttercream.

4 Create a hydrangea directly on top of each cupcake following the instructions on pages 77 to 79. You will require approximately 15 individual flowers to create your hydrangea depending on the size of the individual flowers.

5 To finish, perch a stencilled butterfly on the top of the cupcake and attach it with a fine line of Hydrangea coloured royal icing.

6 Place your cupcakes into cupcake wrappers if required and display on a pretty plate or stand.

stencilled butterflies

1 Using the template on page 94 or your own design, cut a basic butterfly wing shape into a piece of card or thin plastic to create a stencil. You will only need one wing stencil as you can turn it over to create the identical opposite wing.

2 Cut pieces of wax paper large enough for your wing and then spread the royal icing through your stencil using a piece of card or plastic as a spreader. Gently lift the stencil away from the wax paper to leave a clean edge on the wing.

3 Place the wing to one side on a flat surface to dry. Repeat to make as many butterflies as required, making sure you end up with equal numbers of both left and right wings.

4 Fit a silicone piping bag with a no. 2 piping
nozzle or a size appropriate for the wing
you have created. Colour some royal icing with the
liquid food colour of your choice and ²/₃ fill the bag.
Pipe the outline of the wing and tidy up the ends
with a slightly damp paintbrush if needed. Leave
the wings to dry completely for a couple of hours.

5 Remove the wings from the wax paper and
line them up in matching pairs. Cut a piece
of card approximately the size of a business card
and fold it in half: this will be the former on which to
dry your completed butterfly.

6 Re-use a piece of the wax paper that the
wings were dried on and fold it in half, then
lay it into the folded piece of card. Fit a silicone
piping bag with a no. 3 piping nozzle and fill the

bag to ²/₃ with soft-peak royal icing coloured
using the liquid food colour of your choice for the
butterfly body.

7 Pipe a long teardrop of the coloured royal
icing into the crease in the wax paper to
create the butterfly body and then gently insert
the wings into either side of it using the card as
support. Whilst the icing is still wet insert two
flower stamens into the head to give the illusion of
antennae. If the butterflies are going to be eaten,
omit the stamens as they are not edible and
must not be used. Otherwise, safely remove the
butterflies before the cakes are served.

8 Leave the butterflies to dry for several hours
before attaching them to your project with a
small bulb of royal icing.

poinsettia

edibles

SK Instant Mix Royal Icing

SK Professional Dust Food Colour: Poinsettia (Christmas red)

SK Professional Liquid Food Colour: Poinsettia (Christmas red)

SK Sugar Florist Paste (SFP): Daffodil (yellow)

equipment

Card or thin plastic for stencils

Poinsettia cutters (FMM)

Craft knife

Wax paper

Curved former such as a rolling pin

Piping bags

Piping nozzle: no. 2 (PME)

Food-grade foam sponge pieces or kitchen paper

Find paintbrush (SK)

1 Make your own stencils for the poinsettia from card or plastic by drawing around a set of poinsettia cutters or by using a real poinsettia as a template. Once you have drawn the outlines carefully, cut them out with a craft knife.

2 Make up a small batch of royal icing and colour it red using Poinsettia dust food colour to gain the intensity of red required.

3 Cut pieces of wax paper large enough for the individual petals and then spread the royal icing through your stencil using a piece of

card or plastic as a spreader. Slowly lift the stencil away from the wax paper to leave a clean edge on your petals.

4 Whilst the icing is still wet lay the wax paper over a curved surface such as a rolling pin to give the petals a gentle curve. Make several petals of each size plus a few spares to allow for breakages: the number of petals you need will depend on the size of the poinsettia you would like to create. The petals will dry to the touch fairly quickly, however I recommend leaving them for several hours to dry completely before

peeling the wax paper away from the back of the petals.

5 The poinsettia is best assembled directly on top of your cake as it is a very fragile flower. Handling the petals with care, group them into their various sizes. Make up a small amount of red royal icing using Poinsettia dust food colour and place into a piping bag with a no. 2 nozzle.

6 Create a circle of the largest petals on top of the cake and attach them with bulbs of red royal icing. Support the petals with either small pieces of foam or pieces of kitchen paper to dry (remember to remove them before serving).

7 Once the largest petals are in place attach an inner circle of medium petals overlapping

the joins of the first circle. Finally, add one or two small circles of the smallest petals on top of and in between the larger petals. Remember that you can vary the size of your poinsettia depending on the project.

8 Once you have completed the smallest circle of petals brush a little of the red royal icing over the exposed cake covering in the centre of the poinsettia.

9 To finish the flower, roll a number of small yellow balls of Daffodil SFP and stick them into the middle of the poinsettia with red royal icing to represent the centre of the flower. When they are dry paint a small red dot in the centre of each using a fine paintbrush and Poinsettia liquid food colour.

indulgent christmas

For an alternative to the traditional fruit cake, treat your guests to a rich chocolate cake covered in delicious Cocoform Modelling Chocolate and finished with a stunning sugar poinsettia and delicate little pine cones.

iced flowers

1 stencilled poinsettia, see pages 84 to 86

20-22 piped pine cones, see page 91

edibles

20.5cm (8") round chocolate cake

SK White Cocoform Modelling Paste

SK Instant Mix Royal Icing

Sugarpaste: white

SK Sugar Florist Paste (SFP): Bulrush (dark brown) (optional)

SK Professional Liquid Food Colours: Berberis (ivory), Bulrush (dark brown)

SK Professional Dust Food Colour: Bulrush (dark brown)

SK Professional Designer Paste Food Colour: Cream

SK Professional Metallic Lustre Dust Food Colour: Classic Gold

SK Confectioners' Glaze

SK Chocolate Ganache Mix

equipment

20.5cm (8") round cake card

30.5cm (12") round cake drum/board covered with SK White Cocoform Modelling Paste (see pages 14 to 17)

Cocktail sticks

Piping bags

Piping nozzles: nos. 4, 56 (PME)

Small paintbrush

SK Glaze Cleaner (IPA)

Polystyrene block

1 Using your favourite chocolate cake recipe, bake, layer and crumb coat a round cake with chocolate ganache and place it onto a thin cake board equal in diameter to the cake. It is important that your cake is level and has straight sides.

2 Knead the SK White Cocoform well to warm it up; this will make it easier to work with. Roll it out on a surface dusted with icing sugar, cut a disc of the Cocoform to the exact diameter of the cake and lay this on the top of the cake. Roll out the remaining Cocoform into a long strip then, using a sharp knife or cutting wheel, trim it to exactly fit the height and circumference of the cake. Carefully lift the paste and press it lightly into place. Gently rub the join with your fingertips to blend the ends of the paste together.

3 The line around the top edge is concealed in this design with a row of dots piped in cream coloured soft-peak royal icing. Colour the royal icing using a tiny touch of Berberis liquid food colour and place in a piping bag with a no. 4 nozzle. Pipe a series of bulbs around the join keeping them all the same size. If you are new to piping and you are not confident about creating equally sized royal icing dots, firstly cut out small, thin circles of Cocoform using a mini cutter or the tip of a round piping nozzle, attach these around the edge of your cake using royal icing and then pipe your royal icing dots onto them. If your royal icing fills the circle of paste, each dot will appear the same size. Don't forget to use a damp paintbrush to flatten off any peaks left by the piping nozzle before they dry.

4 Cover the cake drum with Cocoform and then cut a hole in the centre to match the diameter of the cake. Carefully place your cake into the central hole using a little ganache to hold the cake board in place.

5 Mix together equal portions of White Cocoform and sugarpaste then roll small balls to create pearls. If the mixture is too soft, seal it in a food-grade plastic bag and allow it to cool in the fridge for a few minutes. Make approximately 70 to 80 balls in various sizes. Paint the pearls with a combination of confectioners' glaze and Classic Gold lustre dust. Clean your paintbrush immediately afterwards with glaze cleaner, then rinse in clean water to preserve your paintbrush.

6 Create pine cones following the instructions on page 91, then attach the gold pearls and pine cones artistically around the base of your cake using bulbs of royal icing or dots of melted white chocolate.

7 Following the instructions on pages 85 to 86, create a red poinsettia in the centre of your Christmas cake. To finish the cake attach satin ribbon around the board in the colour that best complements your event (see page 17).

tutor tip

If your hands are warm and you find that the Cocoform is becoming too sticky to handle, try putting it in the fridge for ten minutes to help it firm up.

mini pine cones

1 These small pine cones are created on cocktail sticks, however their centres can be made from either SFP or royal icing. Firstly smear the ends of all the cocktail sticks with white vegetable fat to prevent sticking.

2 Colour some firm-peak royal icing using Bulrush dust food colour.

3 If you wish to create the pine cone centres from paste, roll a small cone of SFP in your palm and then insert the cocktail stick into it. If you are creating the centre from royal icing, fit a silicone piping bag with a no. 4 nozzle and fill it to $^2/_3$ with the brown royal icing. Insert the cocktail stick into the end of the nozzle then pipe a bulb of royal icing whilst slowly withdrawing the cocktail stick, tapering it off to a point.

4 To prevent the pine cone from slipping down the cocktail stick leave the cone centre to dry overnight; this will give you better results when you come to pipe the pine cones. Push the cocktail sticks into a block of polystyrene for drying.

5 Fit a silicone piping bag with a no. 56 petal nozzle and fill it $^2/_3$ full with the Bulrush coloured royal icing. At the tip of the cone, pipe a small spiral as you would for a rose bud (see page 21), then work your way down the remainder of the cone, piping overlapping petals. This will create the look of a pine cone.

6 Return the cocktail sticks to the polystyrene block to dry overnight. When they are fully dry twist each one slightly to release the pine cone from the cocktail stick.

There is a variety of leaf nozzles on the market, however the two I find most useful are the no. 50 nozzle for miniature leaves and the no. 52 nozzle for average-sized leaves and larger. As royal icing leaves are not normally dusted, extra dimension can be added to them by making two shades of green icing. By filling one side of the piping bag with one shade and the opposite side with the other, you can pipe two-toned leaves for a more realistic finish. This works equally as well for piping a calyx onto the back of a rose or other flower.

A leaf nozzle has a larger V shaped notch on either side of its tip which will form the blades of the piped leaf. The smaller V shaped notch on the upper and lower sides of the tip will form the vein on the leaf.

piped leaves

edibles

SK Instant Mix Royal Icing

SK Professional Liquid Food
Colours: Holly/Ivy, Leaf Green or
another green of your choice

equipment

Piping bag

Leaf nozzle: no. 50 or 52

Fit a silicone piping bag with a leaf piping nozzle then ²/₃ fill the bag with soft-peak green royal icing, two-toned if desired (see above).

Basic leaf: To make a basic leaf, rest the tip of the leaf nozzle on the surface of your cake where you wish the leaf to be placed and apply pressure to your piping bag. When the leaf has reached the required width, stop the pressure and gently pull the nozzle away from the end of the leaf: this will give you a sharp point if your royal icing is the correct consistency.

Calyx: To create a calyx, follow the same method for the basic leaf and pipe five tiny leaves on the back of a flower.

Serrated leaf: To make a serrated leaf, rest the tip of the leaf nozzle on the surface of your cake where you wish the leaf to be placed. Apply pressure to your piping bag to start the leaf, then when it has reached the required width, gently pump the tip of the nozzle in and out whilst elongating the leaf. To finish, stop the pressure and gently pull the nozzle away from the end of the leaf: this will give you a sharp point if your royal icing is at the correct consistency. When creating a spray of piped roses on a project, grouping this type of leaf in a cluster of five will represent a rose leaf.

templates

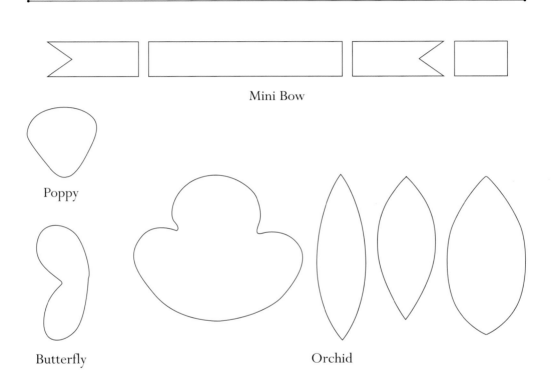

Mini Bow

Poppy

Butterfly

Orchid

suppliers

Squires Kitchen, UK
3 Waverley Lane
Farnham
Surrey
GU9 8BB
0845 61 71 810
+44 1252 260 260
www.squires-shop.com

Squires Kitchen International School
The Grange
Hones Yard
Farnham
Surrey
GU9 8BB
0845 61 71 812
+44 1252 260262
www.squires-school.co.uk

Squires Kitchen, France
+33 (0) 1 82 88 01 66
clientele@squires-shop.fr
www.squires-shop.fr

Squires Kitchen, Italy
www.squires-shop.it

Squires Kitchen, Spain
+34 93 180 7382
cliente@squires-shop.es
www.squires-shop.es

SK stockists

Jane Asher Party Cakes
London
020 7584 6177

Blue Ribbons
Surrey
020 8941 1591

Lawsons Ltd.
Devon
01752 892543

The Sugarcraft Emporium
Worcestershire
01527 576703

Surbiton Art & Sugarcraft
Surrey
020 8391 4664

SK distributors, UK

Confectionery Supplies
Herefordshire
www.confectionerysupplies.co.uk

Guy Paul & Co. Ltd.
Buckinghamshire
www.guypaul.co.uk

Culpitt Ltd.
Northumberland
www.culpitt.com

Australia & New Zealand

Zoratto Enterprises
New South Wales
+61 (2) 9457 0009

Sweden

Tårtdecor
Kungälv
www.tartdecor.se

Manufacturers

Smeg UK Ltd.
www.smeguk.com
www.smeg50style.co.uk

Italian appliance manufacturer
Smeg produces distinctive domestic
appliances combining design,
performance and quality.